This book is about adventure, exploring, finding rare endangered species and how local, regular people can help.

This book is dedicated to Nick Martin - the best wild animal detective around - Judy Soule of the Michigan Natural Features Inventory (MNFI), the good people of Camden Michigan and Steuben County, Indiana, the Michigan Nature Association (MNA), Jeffrey Bednarsh and Dr. Patrick Rusz of William James College of the Grand Valley State Colleges (now GVSU), Dentist David S Brown, Martha Shauer, Dr. Craig Adler of Cornell University, and many others who assisted, cared and helped make the activities documented in this book possible.

It is especially dedicated posthumously to medical Dr David Brown Sr, Vic and Betty Haughey -pronounced "Hoy" - and Helen Skelton.)

I0428681

Chapter One..

After 20 years of working in people's causes, projects, community and program organizing, I do believe I'd had enough.

I went back to school, to get my fifth University degree.

This fifth degree had nothing to do with court pleas or interrogation!

Walking across Michigan States' expanded, newer, treeless brick bomb shelter campus - like cold buildings - some looked like brick cemeteries - as cold as the high winds in winter - very cold , asking myself, "Why am I here?", I turned my face into and against the cold winds, saying, "I am going to keep on and work with the animals." I kept on walking. I didn't look back....

Chapter Two

So, moving away from people, cities, causes and work, I went to study and learn from the animals. The total other.

When graduated, somehow I was most interested in endangered species.

What makes them endangered?

Why are they almost gone?

Geez, even big cats and all our zoo animals were disappearing, even common frogs.

At least the animals are honest.

Most of us are and were afraid of wild animals. Maybe it's wildness that we fear, something here long before us and still, and we can't control it all, despite all the relentless logging, digging, shooting, spraying, mowing. killing, bombing, constructing, land-clearing and pesticide use.

"Nae man can tether time or tide." (Robert Burns) Time nor tide can we control.

Are you proud of eradicating animals from your

areas? Are you proud of it?.

Hawks, eagles, other raptors and other birds, wolves, bears, cougars, buffaloes, eagles , bats, frogs, snakes, moles, earthworms, cats, dogs - get a grip!

Why are we so scared?

Chapter Two

At age 41, after earning my fifth college degree, this time to work with animals, I met Nick Martin.

He was obsessed with endangered snakes, to find them in the wild.

Snakes, whaa?

Many people have a major phobia, some unable to see even one without hysteria, about them, so I had to think if it were worth the effort.

Some say, "I don't like snakes." Translating, that common phrase means that they are afraid of them, even phobic. The phrase is not about snakes but about them.

I had a special interest in animals, from my boyhood experiences and on.

Nick wanted to search for one endangered species - a copperbelly water snake - Whaa???

Chapter Three

He had heard a rumor that an endangered, rare, harmless copperbelly water snake may have bitten a farm girl in Indiana. Surprisingly, the family did not kill it and kept it.

They called a well-known, retired local nature expert nearby - Helen Skelton, - who called up a collector in Ft. Wayne, Indiana, whose owner told Nick.

What were the odds of that?

Nick and I went to Fort Wayne.

It was a copperbelly !

In a cage, it looked beautiful to me but ugly and scary to Nick, and the caged animal was not a happy camper.

"A snake in a cage is biologically dead." (Craig Weatherby, Adrian College, 1982)

Chapter Four

Nick and I went to the area where the snake was found, searching around there. We focused on waterways, streams, ponds, ditches and ponds. We walked up the farm drains and explored the nearby ponds, streams, ditches, fields and farms.

With Helen's help, we went to all the possible habitats all over the county.

Wherever we went, she watched us searching a site, coughing a lot, having a hard time breathing and talking, hoarsely but breathlessly saying, "Snakes will never be protected in Indiana. That'll be the day."

We searched the whole county!

Chapter Five

When we went back to the farm where the snake was first found, exploring a farm drain near the confirmed farm site, two teen farm girls in halter tops drove down in a pickup truck and asked us, "Are you looking for a rare snake?"

Aghast, we said, "Yes, we're looking for the rare copperbelly water snake."

They said that about four years ago, some people from the Toledo Zoo came there to the area and left with bags of snakes.

Nick mused on that. Then he said, "The snake was about to be listed as an endangered species in Ohio. They came to the Indiana/Ohio line to catch some before it became illegal to have them in Ohio. New laws don't look back."

We started to wonder if there were any copperbellies left.

Chapter Six

Then the girls said, "We were cleaning up the hay/manure pile in the barn a few years ago, and two big red-belly black snakes slid out and went outside."

We mused and Nick said, "Hay/manure piles are warm and retain heat."

We wanted to know when, and they said, "We were off school then, so maybe it was around Easter time."

We went up the road to their farm and searched the barn, even the hay/manure piles (ugh). Then Nick said, as he would, "We're losing light." So we searched all around the barn and even nearby where the cows were, even though there were electric fences.

Nick happened to get zapped by one fence, and I could not help but laugh inside, because he was so obsessive, compulsive and demanding, like a control freak. But he was an absolute genius of a detective.

We came up empty, except garter snakes, like we had at most of the other places we explored, where we had also seen ribbon, northern water, brown, blue racers and red king "milk" snakes. None were poisonous.

At least we finally knew where to focus our search.

Chapter Seven

We left for home, but came right back after a few days. We searched every ditch, dredged stream, and all the other possible places in the area. We did not collect any of the snakes we found.

Commercial collectors, some mass collectors - poachers - devastate any secure cover areas and objects and leave a 100% trail of amateur pillage. They collect everything they find for the pet trade. They are lower than rats and as some would say ironically, than snakes.

Back at the original site, toward evening, as Nick would say, 'We're losing light".

Another pickup truck came down the road and Nick, always unabashed, asked them, "Have you seen any rare snakes around here, any 'redbelly black snakes'??'" (the local name).

The young guys - young locals - in the truck said, "Yes we have." Nick perked and asked, "Where?"

"We see them back in those woods in the Spring when we go searching for morel mushrooms."

We became transfixed.

We briefly searched part of the woods.

It was a big woods, we couldn't see the end of it, with a lot of swamps.

At dusk, tired and done, we sat roadside on the edge of the woods on a large pile of wood chips by and in a small swamp.

Excited, but coming up empty, we drove back home.

Chapter Eight

A month later, in July, we drove to the site again. The weather was not with us when we arrived. It was cold, windy and rainy.

We felt it was no use searching, except under cover items where snakes may be seeking refuge - dumped appliances, auto parts, batteries, toilets, dead pigs, junk and garbage piles, debris piles, heavy thatch, rock piles and others.

People throw all kinds of things into a swamp, along roads, even into rivers.

After all this time, we came up empty. Where are they?

What would you do? What would you try more than we did?

Toward sundown, we sat down on the wood chip pile, ready to give up. Despite Nick's being obsessive and focused, we were leaving, resigned to try again maybe next Spring, if at all.

We could not solve the mystery.

Where were they?

END OF PART ONE

PART TWO

Chapter Nine:

Just before getting up and leaving, probably for good, Nick saw that the roadside pile had a lot of holes and that the wood chip pile had layers.

He picked up the top layer, and BOOM, there was an adult copperbelly. He caught it. On further investigation, lifting up other layers, many other snakes would zip out and disappear into the dark, turbid swamp water.

There was no seeing them once they went in....

We had solved the mystery!

Two others were caught in the chip pile.

We started to call the snake "Coppers", and the wood-chip pile, "The Lodge."

Chapter Ten

All three Nick took home and kept them in separate cages.

He was meticulous and kept their cages clean, with the cage tops were of nylon mesh, not metal, which if they probed such a top, always wanting to escape, could give them "mouth rot", deadly to snakes.

Further, he put a small amount of a square of DeCon on top to keep any mites and other parasites off and if there, dead.

He never left them sitting in their own feces, monitoring them closely.

He fed them in a large square shallow bowl, their water drinking bowl, putting small minnows and an occasional salamander into it. He also added calcium into their diet, to keep their bones strong and developing.

He emptied and cleaned the water bowl daily, leaving it sit so the City chlorine would evaporate.

The large female gave birth to a brood of thirteen. He over-wintered them to give them a "head start" for release the next Spring. The two other adults, with the mother and the young were released the next Spring, all at the same site.

Part III

Chapter Eleven

We went to the site again in September. The swamp was dry. We found none in the chip pile.

Nick, always the optimist, started searching in the woods near the swamp, and in a few minutes it seemed, he said, "Copper!"

He had caught a large adult, and showed me its bright orange belly. He caught it on the edge of the woodlot, right by a farmer's bean field.

We then walked down on the edge of the woods by the bean field, and BOOM, Nick caught two more! They were large adults, 4' at least. One was near a shed skin.

We walked all the ½ mile edge along and down to a farm ditch. We went down around the grassy hill banks of the ditch, saw the grass moving, and Nick caught three more large coppers.

We noticed that the ditch was almost dry, but there were isolated pools of trapped catfish and frogs. The coppers were in the tall grass around those pools.

We had found them and saw that it was a colony of coppers. They were hunting together! They were all large females. They had probably been gravid, having just given birth, shedding skins and eating before hibernation.

Where were the males, juveniles and young of the year?

We had solved the mystery, but one mystery leads to another... .

END OF PART THREE

PART FOUR

Chapter Eleven

In 1980 - 82, in Michigan, there were no funds to find endangered species, except for the perennial Kirtland's warbler. There was money only there and for a few plants.

In 1982, I volunteered to search in Michigan for the rare reptiles and amphibians - snakes, turtles, salamanders, sirens, etc.

There were no other takers. I was out there on a wing and a prayer in August 1982. I had only county maps and the historic records. There were maybe five records where they had been found, but the unmapped records were like "in Cass County", "1952", or such vagueness, in other counties and none with specific and detailed localities.

Most of them were considered extinct in the State.

I was on my own, in August, no grant $$, driving and sleeping in my little Honda Civic hatchback.

I had to do a "windshield survey", from the roads only, marking possible sites on a county map.

I searched everywhere at or near or close to the few vague county records.

I went to at least 90 sites and found none. I walked through all the possible habitats - or what were left of them.

Chapter Twelve

Then I started talking with the local residents all over and early morning cafes I stopped at bait stores, local gathering spots, bars, businesses, even local arcades, people on the small town streets and nearby residents.

One lead led me to look up and visit a man who had a camp and cottage area - "the Highlands."

A retired rural mail deliverer, Vic Haughy (pronounced "Hoy") happened to be there and he took interest.

He gave me three local leads from his experiences in the 1950's.

I checked them out, but only found one, a large female. It was on a branch on a stick pile, stretched out on it, completely straight, with no curves, on the edge of the woods, near a small stream and river. What camouflaged cover !

It was too late in the season to find any more ones and certainly not many.

I took her to the Camden café to show them the animal. They were really good people. Some - only the older people - said, "We've seen that one somewhere before."

I asked, "where?" They were vague about that location question, but did say that they used to see them, but not for a long time.

The younger outdoorsmen I met, especially Brian Solomon, and asked had no reports, no leads, even though they were energetic and went to a lot of outdoor areas.

One of the Camden cafe customers took pictures of her with me holding, showing the bright red-orange underside.

The café owner put that picture on the front bulletin board. I was surprised but glad ! Maybe more leads could come from the picture of seeing the animal.

Some asked around town, especially Vick Hoy, and then in mid-Fall sent me a letter:

"Sposed to be a lot of them 'red-belly blacksnakes' out at a man's cottage and lake", with a crude map.

Vic did not have to tell me. It was entirely on his own.

Chapter Thirteen

I surveyed that area to find where key swamp wetlands were and the woods around there, as well as the lake, so as to know where to go in the next Spring.

It was wild and backwoods there, with no neighbors anywhere in sight.

There had been no development nor even much farming there for at least 50 years, if not longer. Even the main road to and from that area had signs saying, "Rough Road Ahead."

Chapter Fourteen

That lead from Vic Hoy was all I had except the area where I had caught the adult female.

WWYHD - What would you have done?

If I found out from other sources that they were here or there, if I found any, I had to call in the State researchers.

End of PART FIVE

PART SIX

Chapter Fifteen

I had to prove that though the next Spring.

Then it became even more interesting....

In late May 1983, the State folks met me there around 9 AM, in the same small town café where people, including Vic Hoy, had given me leads. Vic and Betty were there and sat with us.

The photo of me with the copper was still on the bulletin board.

As we were leaving, Vic said to me, "There are an awful lot of them there (at "Doc's Lake area.").

All I had then were the three sites - based on locals' leads in Michigan, having only found one copper the previous Fall. I had not reported Doc's area yet because I had not found any there last Fall.

There are reasons why the snakes are where they are in the wild, and especially rare, endangered ones. There are also reasons why they are not or no longer at a potential or former site.

Chapter Sixteen

It was the first warm day that Spring, around 70 degrees.

We went out to search three of my reported lead sites.

The first two sites produced no sightings, despite our hard searching.

We went to the third site, where I had found the adult female copperbelly last Fall.

We walked for maybe a mile along a river, with little key habitat present. There were past signs of beaver activity along the river.

The day was clouding over. As the day was getting later, around 4 PM, and as they looking at their watches, we arrived into the area where I had found the copper. I said, "Now here we are getting into the right habitat".

It was floodplain forest, with brush and debris piles, after Spring flooding. My gut was in my throat. Last chance to prove it. I was scared and doubtful.

Chapter Seventeen

Then I saw it!

I said, frozen, "Copper!", pointing motionlessly. I had seen the copper reddish-orange coloration.

They slowly came toward the pile differing angles. The key person - Judy Soul - was behind me. I was transfixed.

Then I had doubts. I saw no movement, and said, "It may be just a leaf". Judy said, "No, I saw it move."

Paul slowly moved up behind the stick pile and pinned the snake's head with a "snake hook". Then I rushed up and caught it. It was a copper!!

Whhhhhhhhhhheeeeeeeeeeeeeeeeeeeeeeeeeeeeewww wwwwwwwwwwwwwwwww

We examined it and then let it go, Judy saying, "I think we've harassed it enough."

It went into a nearby brush pile.

Even its going into a brush pile rather than into the water further confirmed that my written reports were correct - that it was a swamp-forest animal, not needing an immediate water refuge.

Out on a wing and a prayer, paid nothing, the existence of a copperbelly water snake, not extinct nor extirpated, still lives in Michigan.

END OF PART SIX

PART SEVEN

Chapter Eighteen

The next day, what I saw was historic.

It had been a very cold spring in 1983 - highs in the 50's max, rainy and windy. I used that time to search habitats in or near the vague report sites that had at least some life, such as at least turtles and frogs.

Around May 17th, it warmed up into the low 70's. Then there was finally full sun on the next day. I knew where to go immediately. I drove fast to the lead site, thanks to the main lead from Vick Hoy.

Doc had a large lake excavated from 2 swamps, as early as the 1960's, 20 + years ago.

I went immediately by the lake and went directly beyond to a small, open shrub swamp over the wooded hill and down through briars and buckthorn shrubs.

Seeing the shrub swamp from a distance, I moved very slooooooooowly. Staying low and moving very slowly, I came very slowly through the brush right to a side of the swamp, not moving.

Chapter Nineteen

I saw two small flat heads go down underwater right on the edge, not those of frogs or turtles. I froze.

I was kneeling down, staying motionless for at least 15 minutes....

Then I saw it!

Something cut the surface of the quiet water in the swamp middle and started slowly swimming across the surface. I slowly brought up my binoculars and saw that it was a large adult copper!

I still froze.

Then I saw a young adult, a smaller copper adult, maybe of 3 feet, swimming underwater and surface just to my right. I had my camera ready and brought it up very slowly. I took a photo of it Then the two little heads surfaced, and I caught one.

It was a juvenile copperbelly!

I was spellbound seeing the snakes swimming all around the shallow edges barely under water of that small swamp, with heads with mouths open, moving back and forth. Even some common water snakes were moving with them. Words cannot describe it.

I wanted to stay there all day, marveling, seeing and photographing.

No one else reported, recorded nor written about this sight before or since.

They were all around in full activity, very hungry after a cold spring. I caught one of them, a 42" young adult. I kept the two in my pillow case, but still remained motionless or moving very slooooowly.

Said before above, what I was seeing and saw was historic, as nobody else had seen before, or written about anything like an entire colony in motion, nor since.

Again, I wanted to stay there all day, watching without moving. Hunger, mosquitoes, deer biting flies and other pests did not stray my attention as I tuned them all out, not bothering with any pains or pangs.

Chapter Twenty

I had to catch some and photograph them to validate my sightings. I was an unproven volunteer to the State, not an official "researcher." Who cares?

After watching all of the activity, because I had to try at three other sites, I slowly left, asking Doc to take photos of the two snakes, which he did.

I should not have left, so rare and exciting as this found colony all moving together, of all age/size classes.

Maybe I thought I could come back and see them going on as I saw.

I tried but did not see anything like that in all my 18 years of searching, even Midwest-wide.

I went to other lead sites in that county, but had no sightings.

Later I had to call a biologist to come see what I had found. It had rained overnight. The next morning, he and I confirmed the site with photos, one a classic with an adult basking on limb of a shrub.

It became official!!!

For better or for worse....

END OF PART SEVEN

PART EIGHT & 3/8THS:

What happened later and the next years will be in the next book. +